My First Book about the Alphabet of Dangerous Animals

Amazing Animal Books Children's Picture Books

By Molly Davidson

Mendon Cottage Books

I0439609

JD-Biz Publishing

Read More Amazing Animal Books

Purchase at Amazon.com

Download Free Books!
http://MendonCottageBooks.com

Introduction

Animals can be dangerous for several reasons, but they usually do not harm predators or humans without a reason.

Humans may threaten them, their territory, or their babies; these could be causes for the animal to attack.

 is for an African Lion.

African lions are the only cats that live in groups, they are called prides.

It is reported that they killed over 70 people in Tanzania, Africa every year.

A is also for an African Buffalo.

African buffalo, also known as Cape buffalo, weigh up to 1.5 tons!

They use their sharp horns to charge and gore humans and lions who try to eat them.

Their horns can be as tall as 5 1/2 feet.

B is for a Brazilian Wandering Spider.

Brazilian wandering spiders are the World's most venomous spiders.

Humans that are bitten rarely die, thanks to anti-venom, but they are in lots of pain.

They can grow to be about 6 inches across from the tip of one leg to the other.

C is for a Cone Snail.

A cone snail can kill 20 humans in a few minutes, with only one drop of their venom!

They use a long tooth, like a dart, to inject the toxin into their prey, which paralyzes it, so the snail can then eat it.

C is also for a Crocodile, especially the Saltwater Crocodile.

Saltwater crocodiles are the largest living reptile, growing to be 17 feet long and weighing 1,000 pounds.

They have a super strong down bite, and swallow their food whole

D is for a Dendrobatidae, the scientific name for a Poisonous Dart Frog.

Poisonous dart frogs are only 2 inches long, but have enough venom to kill 10 grown men!

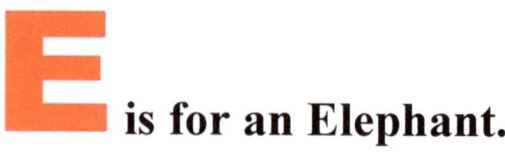 **is for an Elephant.**

Elephants are the largest land animals, weighing 16 tons or 32,000 pounds!

They kill over 500 people per year, usually by trampling or goring them.

 is for a Falcon.

Falcons are not harmful to humans, but they are extremely deadly to their prey.

They sit high up in trees or on cliffs watching for prey, then they swoop down, at up to 200 mph, and snatch their prey without it even having a chance to escape.

G is for a Giant Pacific Octopus.

A Giant Pacific Octopus is the largest octopus on the planet, some measuring 15 feet across.

They will attack and eat sharks, and many other sea creatures, they bite into their prey with their hard beak, and inject a compound that paralyzes and starts eating the flesh away.

G is also for a Great White Shark.

Great white sharks can grow to weigh 5 tons and measure 18 feet long.

They are deadly to their prey, using their super sharp teeth to tear them apart, but more people are killed by dogs each year than by sharks.

 **is for a Hippopotamus.**

Hippos are known as Africa's most deadly animal to humans.

They can get very aggressive for no reason; they will turn over boats in the water and charge at a person, running up to 30 mph.

I is for an Inland Taipan.

An Inland Taipan is the World's most venomous snake; just one bite is strong enough to kill 100 adult men, in less than 45 minutes.

They live in the dry desert of Australia, and change from dark brown in the winter to yellow in the summer.

 **is for a Jaguar.**

Jaguars are the largest cats that live on the American continents.

They have very sharp teeth and a powerful jaw.

They are very good swimmers and will chase their prey into the water.

K  is for a King Cobra.

![King cobra rearing up with hood spread on grass]

King cobras are the largest of all venomous snakes on the planet, with enough venom to kill an elephant.

Over 50,000 people die each year from snake bites, most of these are from the king cobra.

L is for a Leiurus Quinquestriatus, the scientific name for a Deathstalker Scorpion.

© **Wikimedia Commons**

The Deathstalker Scorpion is the World's most venomous scorpion, and 75% of all the people that die from scorpions, die from this one.

They live in the deserts of Africa and the Middle East.

 **is for a Mosquito.**

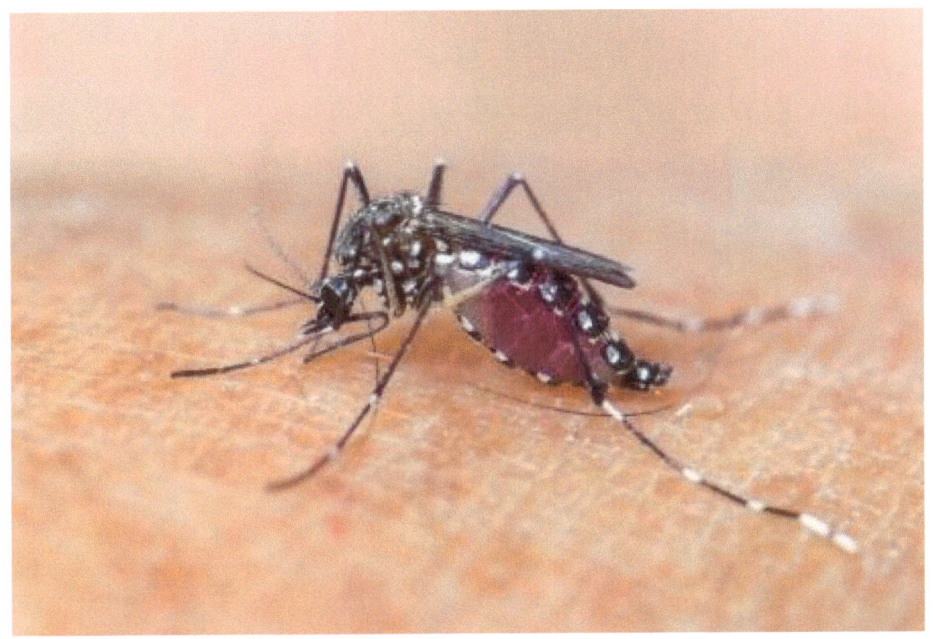

The tiny mosquito is the World's most deadly animal, killing over 2 million people per year.

They transfer diseases to over 70 million people per year, many of which are fatal diseases.

N is for a Neofelis Nebulosa, the scientific name for a Clouded Leopard.

Clouded leopards have the longest teeth of any animal, compared to the size of their skull.

They can run head first down a tree, like a squirrel.

 **is for an Orca.**

Orcas are the fastest moving mammal in the sea, swimming as fast as 31 mph.

They can weigh as much as two elephants!

They eat fish, squid, whales, sea lions, penguins, and polar bears.

P is for a Pufferfish.

When pufferfish are threatened they suck up water which makes them puff up to two times their normal size.

Their spines contain venom that is quite dangerous; it paralyzes its victim causing them to stop breathing.

 **is for a Rattlesnake.**

![Rattlesnake coiled in dry grass]

Rattlesnakes have very powerful venom that they inject into their prey with their two long fangs.

Every time they shed their skin, they grow another rattle segment.

S is for a Stonefish.

Stonefish are the most venomous fish on the planet; their venom causes humans to lose arms or legs, and many times causes death.

They are excellent at camouflaging in with the ocean floor, looking like a rock

S is also for Siafu Ants.

Siafu ants live in groups of up to 50 million.

If one ant is harmed the rest of them swarm in a huge group, as if coming to the rescue.

They dig their teeth into flesh, and will not let go even if their body is ripped in half.

T is for a Tarantula Hawk Wasp.

Astrobradley © <u>Wikimedia Commons</u>

The tarantula hawk wasp is the largest wasp on the planet and they eat tarantulas!

They have one of the most powerful stings of any insect in the World.

U

U is for an Ursus Maritimus, the scientific name for a Polar Bear.

Polar bears are an aggressive bear weighing between 900 - 1,600 pounds.

They could take off a human head with one swipe of their clawed paws.

V is for a Varanus Salvator, the scientific name for a Water Monitor.

Water monitors are one of the largest lizards on Earth, and are very good at swimming, sprinting, and climbing.

They have infecting saliva and an extremely powerful and harmful bite.

 **is for a Wolf.**

Wolves never attack humans, but kill many domesticated animals like cows, chickens, dogs, etc, and if they get really hungry, they will eat sick or wounded wolves.

They can eat 20 pounds of meat at one time.

X is found in one of the World's most deadly animals called the Box Jellyfish.

Box jellyfish have the World's most deadly venom, which attacks the heart, nervous system, and skin cells.

They can have up to 60 tentacles, each up to 15 feet long, and containing enough toxin to kill 50 humans!

Conclusion

I hope you have enjoyed reading about some of the World's most amazingly dangerous animals.

One more fact, most humans that are killed by animals caused the problem, animals just like to be left alone.

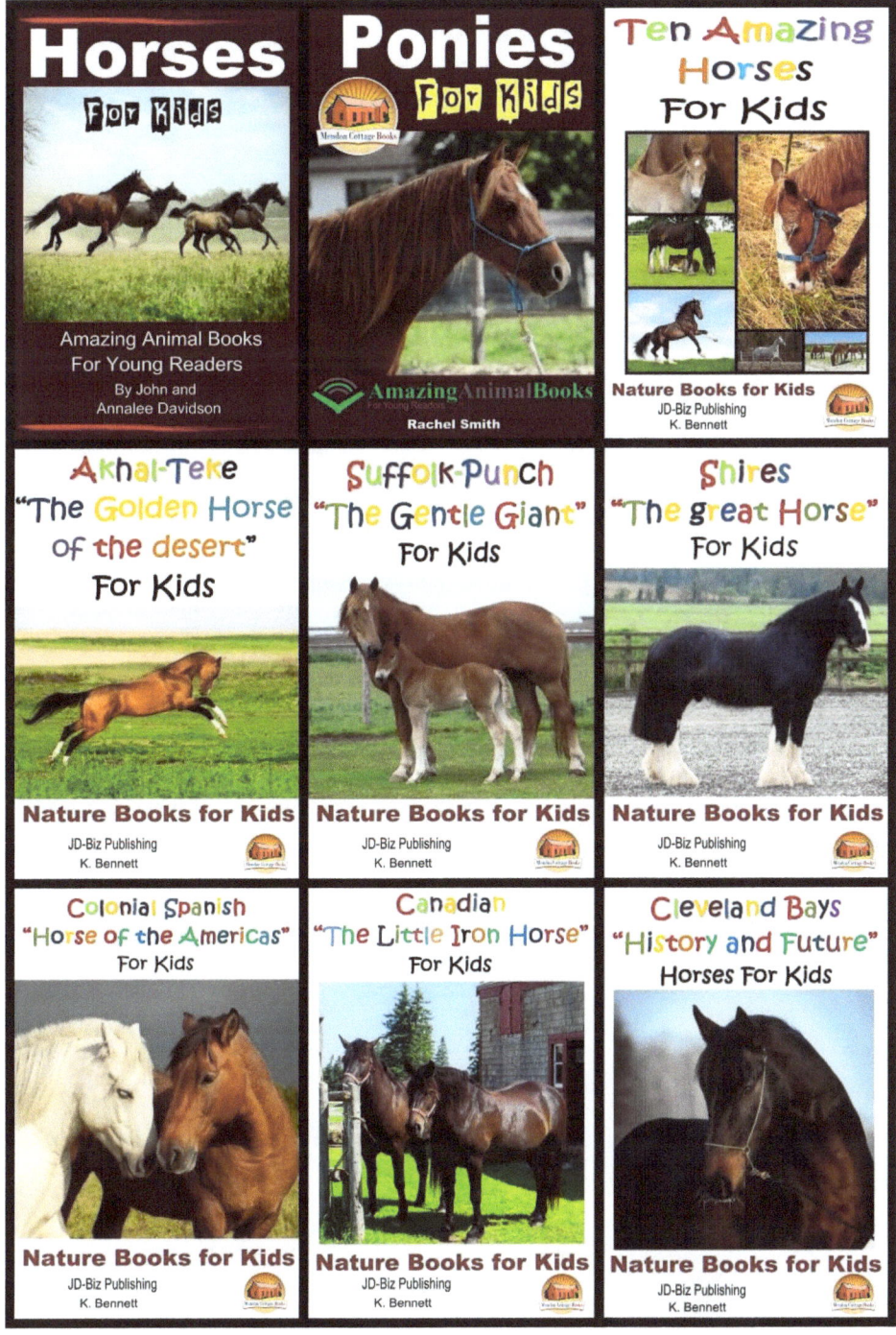

Our books are available at

1. Amazon.com

2. Barnes and Noble

3. Itunes

4. Kobo

5. Smashwords

6. Google Play Books

Download Free Books!
http://MendonCottageBooks.com

Publisher

JD-Biz Corp

P O Box 374

Mendon, Utah 84325

http://www.jd-biz.com/

www.ingramcontent.com/pod-product-compliance
Lightning Source LLC
Chambersburg PA
CBHW050857290526
45792CB00002B/624